The Ultimate Web Development Guide

HTML, CSS, JavaScript and Frameworks for Beginners

Beth Thompson

TABLE OF CONTENTS

Introduction to Web Development

The process of building websites and web applications that are accessible via the internet is known as web development. It combines design, programming, and problem-solving to create digital experiences that are both aesthetically pleasing and useful. From social media sites to e-commerce sites, every website you visit has been created by web developers utilizing a variety of technologies.

From basic static web pages to sophisticated applications with real-time data processing, web development is a broad field. Because of this, developers frequently focus on different areas, like full-stack development, which combines both frontend and backend development.

Web development is constantly changing as a result of new frameworks, libraries, and best practices that enable the creation of quicker, more secure, and interactive websites. The first step to becoming an expert in this fascinating field is learning the basics of web development, regardless of your interest in creating your own website or going into development as a career.

The Definition of Web Development

Web development is fundamentally the process of building, managing, and refining websites and web applications. Writing code, organizing web pages, creating user interfaces, and maintaining databases are all included.

Frontend, backend, and full-stack development are the three main categories into which web development can be separated. Every category is essential to providing a flawless user experience.

A variety of technologies, frameworks, and programming languages are used to create websites. For the front end, the most popular languages are HTML, CSS, and JavaScript; for the back end, backend development frequently uses Python, JavaScript (Node.js), Ruby, PHP, and databases like MySQL or MongoDB.

Web development is an ever-changing field that necessitates ongoing education. For developers to create cutting-edge, effective, and scalable web applications, they must stay current with emerging technologies, industry trends, and best practices.

Full Stack, Backend, and Frontend

The three main categories of web development are front-end, back-end, and full-stack development. Every specialty concentrates on a distinct facet of a website's operation and user interaction.

The term "frontend development" describes the interactive and visual elements of a website that users view and use. Designing a web page's responsiveness, style, and layout is part of it. Languages like HTML, CSS, and JavaScript are used by frontend developers to add interactivity, style elements, and organize content. Libraries and frameworks like React, Vue.js, and Angular are frequently used in frontend development nowadays to produce dynamic and effective user experiences. The primary goal of frontend development is to make sure that websites work and look good on a variety of screens and devices.

A website or web application's server-side logic is the focus of backend development. The processing and storing of data behind the scenes is the responsibility of backend development, whereas frontend development concentrates on what users see. Backend developers create server-side logic and administer databases using programming languages like Python, JavaScript (Node.js), PHP, Ruby, and Java. They simplify backend development by utilizing frameworks such as Ruby on Rails, Django, Laravel, and Express.js. Backend developers make sure that user requests are handled appropriately, databases are used to store and retrieve data effectively, and applications are safe and expandable.

In full-stack development, front-end and back-end development are combined. Full-stack developers can create entire web applications from beginning to end because they are skilled in both areas. They are able to handle everything from designing user interfaces to managing databases and server-side logic because they comprehend the relationship between the frontend and backend. The MERN (MongoDB, Express.js, React, Node.js) or LAMP (Linux, Apache, MySQL, PHP) stacks are two examples of technologies that full-stack developers frequently use to create fully functional web applications.

Every one of these domains is essential to web development, and developers have the option to focus on just one or learn every facet of creating a website or application.

Resources to Help You Get Started

To begin learning web development, you must have the appropriate software and tools to create, test, and publish your projects. These are the fundamental tools to begin with, though your toolkit will change as you advance.

Writing code requires the use of a text editor or an Integrated Development Environment (IDE). Atom, Visual Studio Code, and Sublime Text are popular options. To improve coding efficiency, these editors provide features like auto-completion, syntax highlighting, and extensions. WebStorm and IntelliJ IDEA are examples of advanced IDEs that offer extra features for professional development.

You will need a web browser with developer tools in order to test and debug your web applications. Real-time HTML, CSS, and JavaScript inspection and modification is possible with the built-in developer tools in Google Chrome, Mozilla Firefox, and Microsoft Edge. For debugging and performance analysis, Chrome DevTools is especially well-liked.

For managing code changes and working with others, version control is essential. GitHub, GitLab, and Bitbucket offer platforms for hosting and sharing code repositories, and Git is the most popular version control system. Every web developer must learn Git commands like commit, push, pull, and branch.

You can run your projects on your own computer before posting them to the internet by using a local development environment. Tools such as XAMPP, MAMP, or WAMP facilitate the setup of a local server for PHP application testing, and Node.js makes it possible to run JavaScript on the backend.

Frontend frameworks and libraries, such as React, Tailwind CSS, and Bootstrap, facilitate faster development by offering pre-made styles and components. Using these tools instead of starting from scratch makes it simpler to create user-friendly, responsive interfaces.

Your choice of language will determine the backend technologies you use. When utilizing JavaScript, Node.js and Express.js are popular options. PHP developers use Laravel, whereas Python developers frequently use Django or Flask. One of the most important steps in backend development is setting up a backend environment and connecting to databases such as MySQL or MongoDB.

Software libraries and dependencies are easier to install and manage with a package manager. While pip is used for Python projects, npm (Node Package Manager) is frequently used for JavaScript projects. Package managers make it simple to access open-source libraries, which speeds up development.

You can publish your websites or applications so they are available online by using a deployment platform. For front-end projects, GitHub Pages, Netlify, and Vercel are popular; for back-end applications, Heroku and DigitalOcean are typical. One of the most crucial aspects of web development is knowing how to deploy and maintain websites.

With countless opportunities, web development is a fascinating and fulfilling field. With a basic understanding and the appropriate tools, you can begin developing applications and websites that address real-world issues.

Comprehending the Web and How Websites Function

The internet is a complex system that facilitates communication between billions of devices, enabling everything from cloud computing and online shopping to social media browsing. The information you access when you visit a website is kept on distant computers known as servers, which transmit data to your device via an intricate web of connections.

Fundamentally, the web is a vast collection of websites that are accessible over the internet. The code, pictures, videos, and other media that make up a website are all stored on web servers. The browser uses these files to display a working webpage after your device requests them from the server when you type a URL into your browser.

A number of steps are taking place behind the scenes when a website loads, even though it may appear to happen instantly. Your browser finds the relevant server, requests the required files, and first converts the domain name of the website into an IP address. After receiving the files from the server, the browser transforms them into an organized, aesthetically pleasing page.

Key concepts such as how the internet works, the function of HTTP and HTTPS, how DNS aids in website location, and how browsers interpret and display web pages must all be broken down in order to comprehend how this all works.

The Operation of the Internet

Connecting computers, servers, and other devices worldwide, the internet enables communication and information sharing between them. Since the internet is a decentralized system, no single computer is in charge of it. Rather, it is comprised of millions of interconnected networks that are watched over by governments, businesses, and people all over the world.

In its most basic form, the internet functions by sending data in tiny packets between devices. By utilizing a network of switches and routers, these packets traverse networks, guaranteeing that data gets to its intended location. To enable data transmission and reception, each internet-connected device is given a unique address known as an IP address.

In order to access a website, your device needs to find and connect to the server hosting the website. There are several essential elements in this process.

providers of internet services By giving consumers access to the internet via wired or wireless connections, ISPs serve as gateways. In order to make sure that your requests are delivered to the right places, ISPs route data between your device and the wider internet.

The IP addresses Every internet-connected device has an Internet Protocol IP address, which is a unique identifier. IPv4 and IPv6 addresses are the two varieties.

As the number of connected devices increases, IPv6 employs a longer alphanumeric format, whereas IPv4 uses a numeric format, such as 192.168.1.1.

Transporting Data and Packets The information is divided into tiny packets and sent over the internet separately when you request a webpage. After arriving at their destination, these packets are put back together to guarantee that the full webpage is shown accurately.

Customers and Servers The client-server model is how the web functions. Your device serves as a client, sending data requests to a server, which responds by processing them and returning the required files.

An Overview of HTTP, HTTPS, and DNS

A number of protocols and systems cooperate when you type a web address into your browser to guarantee that the right website is retrieved and safely displayed.

Web browsers and servers communicate with each other using the HTTP Hypertext Transfer Protocol. When you visit a website, your browser asks the web server for certain files, such as an HTML document, images, or scripts, via an HTTP request. After that, your browser receives the requested data from the server.

In order to safeguard data from hackers and other online dangers, HTTPS, or Hypertext Transfer Protocol Secure, is an enhanced version of HTTP. HTTPS makes use of TLS Transport Layer Security or SSL Secure Sockets Layer to guarantee that any information sent between a user and a website is kept private and secure. In the address bar of the browser, websites that use HTTPS show a padlock icon to signify that the connection is encrypted.

In order to convert human-friendly website addresses, such as www.example.com, into numerical IP addresses, such as 192.168.1.1, the DNS Domain Name System is in charge. Given that computers use IP addresses to communicate, DNS serves as a directory that directs browsers to the appropriate server for a particular website.

DNS resolution takes place in a number of steps.

The IP address of the website you are attempting to access is checked by your browser to see if it has already been saved in its cache. The browser asks a DNS resolver if the IP address is not in the cache.

The DNS resolver looks up the domain extension of the website, such as.com or.org, by contacting a root DNS server.

A top-level domain TLD server receives the request and responds with details about the website's authoritative DNS server.

When the DNS resolver receives the correct IP address of the website's server from the authoritative DNS server, it forwards it to the browser.

The browser connects to the web server using the IP address, then requests the files required to show the website.

Without DNS, users would have to memorize lengthy IP addresses rather than straightforward domain names, which would make navigating the web much more difficult.

How Web Pages Appear in Browsers

The final webpage must be displayed by your browser after it has processed and rendered the required files that it has received from the web server. This procedure consists of several steps, such as parsing HTML, using CSS styles, and running JavaScript for interactive elements.

The procedures that go into creating a website include

Understanding HTML Parsing First, the HTML file, which contains the webpage's structure, is read by the browser. In a tree-like structure, it deconstructs HTML into a Document Object Model (DOM), which represents the page's elements.

Utilizing CSS After the DOM is created, the browser formats the page using CSS styles. The website's responsiveness, layouts, colors, and fonts are all controlled by CSS.

The JavaScript execution When a webpage contains JavaScript, the browser interprets and runs the scripts to provide interactive features like form validation, animations, and dynamic content loading.

Making the Page Renderable The browser creates the finished webpage by combining the HTML, CSS, and JavaScript that have been processed. After that, the user's screen is painted with the site's visual representation.

Dealing with Reflows and Repaints Reflow is the term for when the browser must recalculate layouts or repaint portions of the screen when elements change dynamically, like when a window is resized or new content is added.

Modern browsers use methods like caching, preloading resources, and lazy loading images to maximize performance. These methods improve user experience by speeding up page loading times.

Web development students must have a thorough understanding of how websites function, from browser rendering to internet communication. The basis for creating effective, user-friendly, and secure websites is this knowledge.

HTML The Structure of Web Pages

HTML or Hypertext Markup Language is the foundation of every webpage on the internet It provides the basic structure that allows browsers to display text images links and other elements HTML is not a programming language but rather a markup language meaning it is used to structure content rather than execute functions or calculations

HTML works by using a system of elements enclosed in angle brackets These elements define the content of a webpage and help browsers understand how to display it When combined with CSS for styling and JavaScript for interactivity HTML forms the core of modern web development

A web page is essentially a document written in HTML which is interpreted by web browsers to create a visual and interactive experience HTML elements such as headings paragraphs lists and links define the organization and layout of the content While the appearance of a webpage is handled by CSS and its functionality is enhanced by JavaScript HTML remains the backbone of the web

Learning HTML is the first step for anyone interested in web development because it establishes a strong understanding of how websites are structured and how different elements interact

Basic HTML Syntax

HTML follows a simple syntax that consists of elements enclosed in tags Most HTML elements come in pairs with an opening tag and a closing tag The opening tag marks the beginning of an element while the closing tag indicates the end of that element Some elements are self-closing meaning they do not require a closing tag

A basic HTML document consists of several key components The doctype declaration tells the browser what version of HTML is being used The html element serves as the root of the document and contains all other elements The head section contains metadata such as the title character encoding and linked stylesheets The body section contains the actual content of the webpage including text images and links

Here is a simple HTML document structure

```html
<!DOCTYPE html>
<html lang="en">
<head>
    <meta charset="UTF-8">
    <meta name="viewport" content="width=device-width, initial-scale=1.0">
    <title>My First Webpage</title>
</head>
<body>
    <h1>Welcome to My Website</h1>
```

```
    <p>This is a simple webpage created using HTML</p>
</body>
</html>
```

The doctype declaration ensures that the document is interpreted correctly by modern browsers The html tag wraps the entire document The head section contains the title of the page which appears on the browser tab The body section holds the content that will be displayed to users

Indentation and spacing are important in HTML to maintain readability and organization While browsers ignore extra spaces and line breaks using proper formatting makes it easier for developers to understand and edit their code

Essential HTML Tags and Elements

HTML consists of a wide variety of elements that define different types of content Some of the most essential elements include

Headings which range from h1 to h6 are used to structure a webpage and indicate the importance of sections The h1 tag represents the main heading while h6 is the least significant

```html
<h1>Main Heading</h1>
<h2>Subheading</h2>
```

```
<h3>Smaller Subheading</h3>
```

Paragraphs use the p tag to structure blocks of text

```html
<p>This is a paragraph of text in HTML</p>
```

Lists can be unordered or ordered An unordered list ul displays bullet points while an ordered list ol displays numbered items List items are wrapped in li tags

```html
<ul>
    <li>Apples</li>
    <li>Bananas</li>
    <li>Cherries</li>
</ul>

<ol>
    <li>Step One</li>
    <li>Step Two</li>
    <li>Step Three</li>
</ol>
```

Links are created using the anchor a tag The href attribute specifies the destination URL

```html
<a href="https://www.example.com">Visit Example</a>
```

Images are embedded using the img tag The src attribute specifies the image location and the alt attribute provides alternative text for accessibility

```html
<img src="image.jpg" alt="A beautiful sunset">
```

Divs and spans are used to group elements A div is a block-level container while a span is an inline container

```html
<div>
    <h2>Section Title</h2>
    <p>This is a paragraph inside a div</p>
</div>

<p>This is <span style="color: red;">red text</span> inside a paragraph</p>
```

These elements form the foundation of web development allowing developers to structure content in a meaningful way

Forms Tables and Multimedia

Forms allow users to submit information to a website They consist of input fields buttons and other interactive elements The form element wraps input elements and specifies an action attribute to determine where the data is sent

A basic form includes text inputs radio buttons checkboxes and a submit button

```html
<form action="submit-form.php" method="post">
  <label for="name">Name</label>
  <input type="text" id="name" name="name">

  <label for="email">Email</label>
  <input type="email" id="email" name="email">

  <label>Gender</label>
  <input type="radio" id="male" name="gender" value="male">
  <label for="male">Male</label>
  <input type="radio" id="female" name="gender" value="female">
  <label for="female">Female</label>

  <label for="subscribe">Subscribe to newsletter</label>
```

```html
<input type="checkbox" id="subscribe" name="subscribe">

  <button type="submit">Submit</button>
</form>
```

Tables organize data into rows and columns The table element contains rows tr which contain table headers th and table data td

```html
<table>
  <tr>
    <th>Name</th>
    <th>Age</th>
    <th>City</th>
  </tr>
  <tr>
    <td>John</td>
    <td>30</td>
    <td>New York</td>
  </tr>
  <tr>
    <td>Jane</td>
    <td>25</td>
    <td>Los Angeles</td>
  </tr>
</table>
```

```
```

Multimedia elements such as images audio and video enhance user experience The audio element embeds sound files and allows playback controls

```html
<audio controls>
    <source src="music.mp3" type="audio/mpeg">
    Your browser does not support the audio element
</audio>
```

The video element embeds video content

```html
<video controls width="600">
    <source src="video.mp4" type="video/mp4">
    Your browser does not support the video tag
</video>
```

HTML provides the foundation for creating structured content on the web By mastering basic syntax essential tags and interactive elements like forms tables and multimedia developers can build engaging and functional websites

CSS Styling Your Website

Cascading Style Sheets or CSS is the language used to style and visually enhance HTML elements on a webpage While HTML provides the structure CSS controls the appearance including colors fonts spacing layout and responsiveness Without CSS web pages would appear as plain unformatted text with no visual appeal or organization

CSS works by selecting HTML elements and applying styles to them It allows web developers to create visually engaging experiences improve user navigation and ensure consistency across different screen sizes and devices CSS plays a crucial role in making websites more accessible readable and user-friendly

One of the key advantages of CSS is that it separates content from design This means that developers can change the styling of a website without altering its HTML structure making updates and redesigns much easier CSS also enables animations transitions and responsive layouts which are essential for modern web design

CSS Syntax and Selectors

CSS follows a simple syntax where styles are applied to elements using selectors properties and values A CSS rule consists of a selector which targets an HTML element a property which defines what is being changed and a value which specifies the appearance

Example of basic CSS syntax

```
selector {
    property: value;
```

}

For instance to change the text color of all paragraphs to blue you would use

```
p {
    color: blue;
}
```

Selectors in CSS determine which elements are affected by a style rule There are several types of selectors including

Element selectors which target all instances of a specific HTML tag

```
h1 {
    font-size: 24px;
    color: red;
}
```

Class selectors which target elements with a specific class attribute A period (.) is used before the class name

```
.special-text {
    font-weight: bold;
    color: green;
}
```

ID selectors which target a single unique element with a specific ID A hash (#) is used before the ID name

```
#main-title {
    text-align: center;
    font-size: 30px;
}
```

Group selectors which apply the same styles to multiple elements

```
h1, h2, h3 {
    font-family: Arial, sans-serif;
}
```

Descendant selectors which target elements inside another element

```
div p {
    color: gray;
}
```

Pseudo-classes which apply styles based on an element's state such as hovering over a link

```
a:hover {
    color: orange;
}
```

Pseudo-elements which style specific parts of an element like the first letter of a paragraph

```
p::first-letter {
    font-size: 24px;
    color: red;
}
```

CSS selectors are powerful and allow developers to apply styles in a targeted and efficient manner

Box Model and Positioning

The box model is one of the core concepts in CSS Every HTML element is considered a rectangular box consisting of four areas

Content   The   actual   text   or   image   inside   the   element
Padding   The   space   between   the   content   and   the   border
Border   The   outer   edge   surrounding   the   padding
Margin The space between the element and other elements

Visual representation of the box model

```
.box {
    width: 200px;
    height: 100px;
    padding: 10px;
    border: 5px solid black;
    margin: 20px;
```

```
}
```

Positioning in CSS determines how elements are placed within a webpage The position property has several values

Static Default positioning where elements follow the normal document flow

```
div {
    position: static;
}
```

Relative Positions an element relative to its normal position

```
div {
    position: relative;
    top: 10px;
    left: 20px;
}
```

Absolute Positions an element relative to its nearest positioned ancestor or the document itself if no ancestor is positioned

```
div {
    position: absolute;
    top: 50px;
    right: 30px;
}
```

Fixed Positions an element relative to the browser window so it stays in place when scrolling

```
div {
    position: fixed;
    bottom: 0;
    right: 0;
}
```

Sticky Switches between relative and fixed positioning depending on scroll position

```
div {
    position: sticky;
    top: 10px;
}
```

Understanding the box model and positioning is essential for controlling layouts and ensuring elements appear exactly where they are needed

Flexbox and Grid for Layouts

CSS provides two powerful layout systems for organizing elements on a page Flexbox and Grid

Flexbox (Flexible Box) is designed for one-dimensional layouts either in a row or a column It is useful for aligning items distributing space and making elements flexible

Example of a flex container

```
.container {
    display: flex;
    justify-content: space-between;
    align-items: center;
}
```

Key Flexbox properties

display	flex	Enables	flexbox	on	a	container
flex-direction		row	or		column	layout
justify-content		Aligns		items		horizontally
align-items		Aligns		items		vertically

flex-wrap Controls whether items wrap onto multiple lines

Grid is a two-dimensional layout system allowing elements to be positioned in both rows and columns It provides a powerful way to create structured and complex layouts

Example of a grid layout

```
.grid-container {
    display: grid;
    grid-template-columns: 1fr 2fr 1fr;
```

```
grid-template-rows: auto;
    gap: 10px;
}
```

Key Grid properties

display	grid	Enables	grid	on	a	container
grid-template-columns		Defines		column		structure
grid-template-rows		Defines		row		structure
gap	Sets	spacing	between		grid	items
align-items and justify-items Controls alignment within grid cells						

Flexbox is ideal for smaller layout adjustments while Grid is better suited for full-page layouts Combining both provides maximum flexibility and control

Responsive Design and Media Queries

Responsive design ensures that a website looks good on all screen sizes from desktops to smartphones CSS enables responsive design through flexible units and media queries

Flexible units include percentages viewport widths (vw) and viewport heights (vh) as well as em and rem units for scalable typography

Example of flexible width

```
.container {
    width: 80%;
    max-width: 1200px;
```

```
    margin: auto;
}
```

Media queries allow developers to apply different styles depending on the device's screen size

Example of a media query

```
@media (max-width: 768px) {
    body {
        background-color: lightgray;
    }
}
```

Key breakpoints for responsive design

Small	screens	480px	(smartphones)
Medium	screens	768px	(tablets)
Large	screens	1024px	(laptops)

Extra-large screens 1200px and above (desktops)

By combining flexible layouts media queries and adaptive images developers can create websites that adjust seamlessly to any device ensuring a consistent user experience

CSS is an essential tool for web developers enabling them to style elements control layouts and build responsive user-friendly websites Understanding syntax selectors box model positioning Flexbox Grid and media queries empowers developers to create visually appealing and adaptable designs

JavaScript Bringing Pages to Life

Imagine a world where websites never change No animations no buttons responding when you click them no instant updates without refreshing the page It would feel static lifeless But thanks to JavaScript the web is alive and interactive It's the magic behind dynamic content the reason you can scroll through social media see real-time updates and even play browser-based games

JavaScript often called the "language of the web" is what makes websites engaging and responsive While HTML provides the structure and CSS handles the style JavaScript brings functionality Without it the internet would be a much duller place

Whether you want to build interactive forms create animations load data without refreshing the page or even develop full-scale web applications JavaScript is your gateway into the exciting world of web development It's beginner-friendly yet incredibly powerful and widely used across the tech industry

Introduction to JavaScript

JavaScript is a high-level programming language designed for adding interactivity to web pages Originally created in just ten days in 1995 JavaScript has evolved into one of the most powerful and versatile languages in the world Today it runs not just in browsers but also on servers databases and even mobile applications

What makes JavaScript so special

1. It's Everywhere Every modern web browser supports JavaScript allowing developers to write code that runs on billions of devices worldwide

2. It's Easy to Learn Compared to many other programming languages JavaScript has a forgiving syntax making it accessible for beginners

3. It's Fast Because JavaScript runs directly inside your browser there's no need for slow server-side processing making web pages feel snappy and responsive

4. It's Versatile Whether you want to create a simple interactive webpage build a full-stack web application or even code a mobile app JavaScript can do it all

5. It's Supported by a Huge Community JavaScript has one of the largest developer communities in the world meaning you'll always find help tutorials and libraries to make coding easier

A simple way to see JavaScript in action is by running it in your browser's developer console Open your browser right-click anywhere on the page choose "Inspector "Inspect Element" then go to the Console tab Now try typing

```js
console.log("Hello World");
```

Press Enter and you'll see "Hello World" appear in the console Congratulations you just wrote your first JavaScript program

Variables Data Types and Operators

At the core of JavaScript are variables which store and manipulate data Imagine variables as little containers that hold information which can change as your program runs

Declaring Variables

There are three ways to declare variables in JavaScript

1. `var` The old way of declaring variables (still works but not recommended)

2. `let` The modern way to declare variables that can be reassigned

3. `const` Used for variables that should never be changed

```js
var oldVariable = "I am outdated";

let name = "Alice";

const birthYear = 1995;
```

```
```

Data Types

JavaScript handles different types of data including

1. **Strings** Text values written inside quotes

   ```js
   let greeting = "Hello, world!";
   ```

2. **Numbers** Integers and decimals

   ```js
   let age = 25;

   let price = 19.99;
   ```

3. **Booleans** True or false values

```js
let isStudent = true;
```

4. **Array** Lists of values

```js
let colors = ["red", "blue", "green"];
```

5. Objects Collections of key-value pairs

```js
let person = { name: "Alice", age: 25, job: "Developer" };
```

Operators

Operators in JavaScript allow you to perform calculations and comparisons

1. Arithmetic Operators `+ - * / %`

```js
let sum = 10 + 5; // 15

let remainder = 10 % 3; // 1
```

2. Comparison Operators `== === != !== > < >= <=`

```js
let isEqual = (5 == "5"); // true (loose comparison)

let isStrictEqual = (5 === "5"); // false (strict comparison)
```

3. Logical Operators `&& || !`

```js
let canEnter = (age >= 18 && hasTicket);
```

Variables and operators are the foundation of programming allowing JavaScript to make decisions and manipulate data dynamically

Functions Events and DOM Manipulation

Now that we understand variables let's explore functions events and the Document Object Model (DOM) which allow JavaScript to interact with web pages

Functions The Heart of JavaScript

Functions are reusable blocks of code that perform a specific task Instead of writing the same code multiple times you can define a function and call it whenever needed

```js
function greetUser(name) {

    return "Hello, " + name + "!";

}

console.log(greetUser("Alice")); // Hello, Alice!
```

Events Making Websites Interactive

JavaScript can respond to user actions like clicks keyboard presses or mouse movements These interactions are called events

```js
document.getElementById("myButton").addEventListener("click", function() {

    alert("Button clicked!");

});
```

When the button with the ID "myButton" is clicked JavaScript triggers the alert This is how websites respond instantly to user interactions

DOM Manipulation Changing the Page Dynamically

The Document Object Model (DOM) represents the structure of an HTML page and JavaScript can modify it in real time For example you can change text hide elements or even add new content

```js
document.getElementById("title").innerText = "Welcome to JavaScript!";
```

```
```

This line selects the element with the ID "title" and updates its text dynamically

ES6+ Features Let Const Arrow Functions and More

JavaScript is constantly evolving and newer versions introduce powerful features ES6 (also known as ECMAScript 2015) brought major improvements making JavaScript cleaner and more efficient

`let` and `const`

Instead of `var` modern JavaScript uses `let` and `const`

```js
let name = "Alice"; // Can be changed

const birthYear = 1995; // Cannot be changed
```

Arrow Functions

A shorter way to write functions

```js
const add = (a, b) => a + b;

console.log(add(5, 3)); // 8
```

Template Literals

Use backticks (`) to embed variables inside strings easily

```js
let name = "Alice";

console.log(`Hello, ${name}!`);
```

Destructuring

Quickly extract values from objects or arrays

```js
let person = { name: "Alice", age: 25 };

let { name, age } = person;

console.log(name, age); // Alice 25
```

Spread Operator

Easily copy or merge arrays and objects

```js
let numbers = [1, 2, 3];

let moreNumbers = [...numbers, 4, 5, 6];

console.log(moreNumbers); // [1, 2, 3, 4, 5, 6]
```

```

JavaScript is what makes the web fun dynamic and alive Mastering JavaScript allows you to build interactive websites automate tasks and even develop full-fledged applications The journey may seem overwhelming at first but with practice and curiosity you'll unlock endless possibilities Welcome to the world of JavaScript where creativity meets technology and where your ideas can come to life with just a few lines of code
```

Version Control with Git and GitHub

Imagine working on a big project—maybe a website or an app You make a few changes and suddenly something breaks You try to undo your edits but now the whole thing is even worse You wish you could just go back to when everything was working perfectly

This is exactly what version control helps with It allows you to track changes save different versions of your work and collaborate with others without worrying about losing progress Whether you're a solo developer working on a personal project or part of a large team building a complex application version control is essential

At the heart of modern version control is Git a powerful open-source tool that keeps track of code changes And to make things even better developers use GitHub a cloud-based platform where they can store manage and collaborate on projects with Git

Understanding Git and GitHub is one of the most valuable skills for any web developer Let's dive in

What is Version Control

Version control also known as source control is a system that helps developers manage changes to their code over time It keeps a history of modifications allowing you to revert to previous versions compare changes and work with others without overwriting each other's work

Why is Version Control Important

Track Changes Every update is recorded so you can see what was modified and who made the change

Undo Mistakes If something breaks you can revert to a previous working version

Collaborate Seamlessly Multiple developers can work on the same project without conflicts

Experiment Safely You can create different branches of a project to test new features before merging them into the main code

Backup Your Work If your computer crashes or you accidentally delete files your code is safely stored in a version control system

There are different types of version control systems but Git is the most widely used because of its speed efficiency and flexibility

Setting Up Git and Basic Commands

Before you can start using Git you need to install it and configure it on your computer

Installing Git

Windows

Download Git from git-scmcom

Run the installer and choose the default settings

Open Git Bash to start using Git

Mac

Open Terminal and type

git --version

If Git is not installed install it using Homebrew

brew install git

Linux

Install Git with your package manager

sudo apt install git For UbuntuDebian

sudo dnf install git For Fedora

Configuring Git

Once Git is installed set up your name and email which will be linked to every change you make

git config --global username "Your Name"

git config --global useremail "youremail@examplecom"

Check your configuration with

git config --list

Initializing a Git Repository

A repository or repo is where Git stores the history of your project To turn a project folder into a Git repository navigate to the folder and run

git init

This creates a hidden git folder where Git will track changes

Tracking and Committing Changes

To save your work Git uses commits Think of a commit as a snapshot of your project at a specific moment in time

Check the status of your files

git status

Add files to be tracked

git add filename.txt Add a single file

git add   Add all changes

Commit the changes with a message

git commit -m "Added a new feature"

Every commit creates a checkpoint allowing you to go back if needed

Viewing Commit History

To see past commits use

git log

For a simplified one-line view

git log --oneline

Undoing Changes

If you make a mistake you can undo changes

Remove changes from staging area before commit

git reset HEAD filename.txt

Undo last commit but keep changes

git reset --soft HEAD~1

Undo last commit and discard changes

git reset --hard HEAD~1

Git allows you to fix mistakes easily without fear of permanently losing work

Collaborating on GitHub

GitHub is an online platform that lets developers store their Git repositories collaborate with others and manage projects efficiently It acts as a backup system and a collaboration tool making it easy to share code with teammates or contribute to open-source projects

Creating a GitHub Repository

Sign up at GitHubcom

Click New Repository

Give it a name and description

Choose Public for open-source or Private for personal projects

Click Create Repository

Connecting a Local Project to GitHub

If you have a project on your computer and want to upload it to GitHub

Navigate to your project folder

Initialize Git if you haven't already

```
git init
```

Add the remote GitHub repository

```
git remote add origin https://githubcom/yourusername/repository-namegit
```

Push the code to GitHub

```
git push -u origin main
```

Now your project is live on GitHub

Cloning a GitHub Repository

If you want to work on a project that's already on GitHub you can clone it to your computer

```
git clone https://githubcom/username/repository-namegit
```

This creates a local copy that you can edit and contribute to

Branching and Merging

Git allows developers to work on different features separately using branches A branch is a copy of the main code where you can make changes without affecting the original project

Create a new branch

git branch feature-branch

Switch to the new branch

git checkout feature-branch

Make changes and commit them

Merge the branch back into main

git checkout main

git merge feature-branch

This allows multiple developers to work on different features simultaneously

Pull Requests and Collaboration

When working with a team on GitHub changes are usually submitted through Pull Requests PRs

Push your branch to GitHub

git push origin feature-branch

Go to your repository on GitHub and click Compare & pull request

Write a description and submit the request

Other team members can review and merge your changes

Pull requests allow for discussion and code review before merging changes ensuring high-quality code

Version control with Git and GitHub is a game-changer for web development It allows developers to keep track of changes fix mistakes easily and collaborate with teams worldwide Learning Git may seem overwhelming at first but once you get comfortable with basic commands you'll realize how powerful and indispensable it is

Whether you're working alone on a personal project or contributing to a large open-source initiative mastering Git and GitHub will make you a more efficient and confident developer Welcome to the world of version control where every line of code is safe backed up and part of a larger journey toward building something amazing

Building Interactive Websites with JavaScript

The magic of modern websites isn't just in their structure or their design It's in the way they respond to users Think about when you fill out a form online and get instant feedback when you scroll through an endless feed of social media posts or when a website remembers your preferences This interactivity is all thanks to JavaScript

JavaScript allows developers to create dynamic and responsive websites that can react to user actions communicate with web services and store data locally It's what turns a basic web page into a full-fledged application Understanding how to handle forms interact with APIs and manage local storage is essential for anyone looking to build professional web experiences

Handling Forms and User Input

Forms are one of the most common ways users interact with websites Whether it's signing up for an account filling out a contact form or searching for something forms need to be interactive responsive and user-friendly JavaScript helps in validating inputs providing real-time feedback and submitting data

Capturing Form Inputs

In JavaScript you can access form elements using the Document Object Model DOM Here's how to capture user input from a text field

```js
const nameInput = documentgetElementById("name")

nameInputaddEventListener("input" function(event) {
  consolelog("User typed " eventtargetvalue)
})
```

This code listens for input events on the text field and logs whatever the user types

Form Validation

Ensuring users enter correct data is crucial You don't want an empty email field or an incorrectly formatted phone number JavaScript helps validate inputs before submitting the form

```js
const form = documentgetElementById("signup-form")
const emailInput = documentgetElementById("email")

formaddEventListener("submit" function(event) {
  if (!emailInputvalueincludes("@")) {
    alert("Please enter a valid email address")
```

```
    eventpreventDefault() // Prevents the form from submitting
  }
})
```

This prevents a form submission if the email is invalid making the user correct their input before proceeding

Adding Real-Time Feedback

Instead of waiting until submission you can provide instant feedback to guide users

```js
emailInputaddEventListener("input" function() {
  if (emailInputvalueincludes("@")) {
    emailInputstyleborderColor = "green"
  } else {
    emailInputstyleborderColor = "red"
  }
})
```

This changes the border color of the input field based on whether the user has entered a valid email making the experience smoother

Working with APIs and Fetch

The web is full of APIs that allow websites to fetch and send data in real time Want to display weather updates fetch user profiles from a database or show trending news JavaScript can retrieve this data using the Fetch API

Making a Simple API Request

Fetching data from an API is straightforward using JavaScript's Fetch API

```js
fetch("https://api.example.com/data")
  then(response => responsejson())
  then(data => consolelog(data))
  catch(error => consoleerror("Error fetching data " error))
```

This code sends a request to the API converts the response into JSON and logs it If something goes wrong the catch block handles the error

Displaying API Data on a Webpage

Let's say you want to display a list of users from an API Here's how you do it

```js
const userList = documentgetElementById("users")
```

```js
fetch("https://jsonplaceholdertypicodecom/users")
  then(response => responsejson())
  then(users => {
    usersforEach(user => {
      const listItem = documentcreateElement("li")
      listItemtextContent = username
      userListappendChild(listItem)
    })
  })
```

This fetches user data from an API and dynamically adds it to an unordered list on the webpage

Sending Data to an API

Sometimes you need to send data instead of just retrieving it Here's how you submit a form using Fetch

```js
const form = documentgetElementById("contact-form")

formaddEventListener("submit" function(event) {
  eventpreventDefault()

  const formData = {
```

```
      name documentgetElementById("name")value
      email documentgetElementById("email")value
      message documentgetElementById("message")value
  }

  fetch("https://api.example.com/submit" {
    method "POST"
    headers {
      "Content-Type" "applicationjson"
    }
    body JSONstringify(formData)
  })
  then(response => responsejson())
  then(data => consolelog("Form submitted successfully " data))
  catch(error => consoleerror("Error submitting form " error))
})
```

This captures form data sends it to an API and logs a success or error message

Local Storage and Session Storage

Not all data needs to be sent to a server Sometimes you want to store user preferences locally so they don't disappear when the page is refreshed JavaScript provides two main ways to store data locally **Local Storage** and **Session Storage**

Local Storage

Local Storage allows data to persist even after the browser is closed It's great for storing user settings themes or other permanent data

Storing data
```js
localStoragesetItem("username" "JohnDoe")
```

Retrieving data
```js
const username = localStoragegetItem("username")
consolelog(username) // Outputs JohnDoe
```

Removing data
```js
localStorageremoveItem("username")
```

Session Storage

Session Storage is similar to Local Storage but data is only saved while the page is open Once the tab is closed the data is lost

Storing data
```js
```

```js
sessionStoragesetItem("sessionID" "12345")
```

Retrieving data
```js
const sessionID = sessionStoragegetItem("sessionID")
consolelog(sessionID)
```

Clearing session storage
```js
sessionStorageremoveItem("sessionID")
```

Using Local Storage for a Dark Mode Toggle

Here's a practical example of using Local Storage to save a user's theme preference

```js
const themeToggle = documentgetElementById("theme-toggle")

// Check saved theme on page load
if (localStoragegetItem("theme") === "dark") {
  documentbodyclassListadd("dark-mode")
}

themeToggleaddEventListener("click" function() {
```

```
documentbodyclassListtoggle("dark-mode")
const theme = documentbodyclassListcontains("dark-mode") ? "dark" : "light"
localStoragesetItem("theme" theme)
})
```

This ensures that if a user enables dark mode the setting remains even if they refresh the page

Building interactive websites with JavaScript is what makes the web come alive From handling user input and validating forms to fetching data from APIs and storing user preferences locally JavaScript provides the tools needed to create dynamic and engaging web experiences Understanding these concepts is crucial for any web developer looking to build functional and user-friendly applications

Introduction to Web Frameworks and Libraries

When building websites from scratch you quickly realize that while HTML CSS and JavaScript provide the foundation developing complex and interactive applications can become repetitive and time-consuming Imagine writing the same code to manipulate the DOM or handling data updates manually every time a user interacts with your site This is where web frameworks and libraries come in

Frameworks and libraries provide pre-written code that helps developers build web applications more efficiently They streamline common tasks like rendering UI elements managing state and handling user interactions Instead of reinventing the wheel you can use these tools to speed up development improve performance and write cleaner more maintainable code

Why Use Frameworks and Libraries

Faster Development

Frameworks and libraries provide pre-built functions and components that allow developers to build applications quickly Instead of manually coding common features like navigation menus buttons or form validation these tools offer ready-to-use solutions saving time and effort

For example JavaScript frameworks like React Vue and Svelte come with features that handle dynamic content updates automatically You don't have to manually modify the DOM every time something changes in your app The framework does it for you

Better Code Organization

As web applications grow larger managing JavaScript files can become messy and unstructured Frameworks provide a structured approach by breaking the code into reusable components and modules. This makes it easier to maintain and debug complex applications

Improved Performance

Modern frameworks are optimized for performance They use techniques like virtual DOM in React and reactive state management in Vue and Svelte which make applications run faster by updating only the necessary parts of the UI instead of re-rendering the whole page

Cross-Browser Compatibility

Writing plain JavaScript often requires handling browser inconsistencies since different browsers may interpret the code differently Frameworks and libraries handle these issues for you ensuring your app works seamlessly across all major browsers

Community Support and Ecosystem

Popular frameworks have large communities that contribute plugins extensions and third-party tools Whether you need authentication systems state management solutions or UI component libraries you'll find plenty of resources to extend your application's functionality without having to build everything from scratch

Overview of Popular Choices React Vue Svelte

There are many JavaScript frameworks and libraries available but three of the most popular ones are React Vue and Svelte. Each has its own strengths and is suited for different types of projects

React

Developed by Facebook now Meta React is the most widely used JavaScript library for building user interfaces It's known for its component-based architecture and use of the virtual DOM

Key Features of React

Component-Based Development
React applications are made up of reusable components These components are self-contained pieces of UI that manage their own state making it easier to build and maintain complex applications

Virtual DOM

Instead of updating the actual DOM directly React uses a virtual DOM which is a lightweight copy of the real DOM This makes UI updates faster and more efficient because React calculates the minimum number of changes needed and updates only those parts

State Management

React uses state and props to manage data inside components For larger applications external state management libraries like Redux or Context API are often used

Strong Ecosystem

With a massive community React has numerous third-party libraries like **React Router for navigation** and **Material-UI for pre-built components** making development even more efficient

When to Use React

React is ideal for large-scale applications where performance and maintainability are key It's widely used for enterprise applications dashboards and dynamic websites that require frequent updates

Vue

Vue is a progressive framework known for its simplicity and ease of use. Unlike React which is just a library Vue is a full-fledged framework that provides built-in tools for handling UI state transitions and routing

Key Features of Vue

Reactivity System

Vue uses a reactive data binding system meaning that when you update the data the UI updates automatically without needing extra code to manipulate the DOM

Easy Learning Curve

Vue's syntax is beginner-friendly making it easier to pick up than React or Angular It combines HTML CSS and JavaScript in a structured way which makes development more intuitive

Component-Based Architecture

Like React Vue encourages reusable components which makes code organization and maintenance simpler

Built-in Features

Vue comes with Vue Router for navigation and Vuex for state management out of the box reducing the need for third-party tools

When to Use Vue

Vue is perfect for small to medium-sized projects and is popular among startups and solo developers It's great for progressive web apps and interactive single-page applications

Svelte

Svelte is a relatively new framework that takes a different approach compared to React and Vue Instead of updating the DOM in real-time using a virtual DOM Svelte compiles components into highly optimized JavaScript at build time making it one of the fastest frameworks available

Key Features of Svelte

No Virtual DOM
Unlike React and Vue which use a virtual DOM Svelte compiles the code to efficient JavaScript that updates the DOM directly resulting in blazing-fast performance

Simple Syntax
Svelte's syntax is clean and minimalistic making it easy for developers to learn and use Components in Svelte look much like regular HTML CSS and JavaScript files

Smaller Bundle Size
Since Svelte compiles everything down to JavaScript there's no need for an external runtime making the final application much lighter and faster

When to Use Svelte

Svelte is great for performance-critical applications or when you want to build a web app with less boilerplate code. It's especially useful for static sites dashboards and lightweight applications

Setting Up a Basic React Project

Since React is the most popular choice among developers let's walk through setting up a simple React project

Step 1 Install Nodejs and npm

React requires Nodejs and npm to run If you haven't installed them yet download and install the latest version from nodejsorg

Check if Nodejs and npm are installed by running

```sh
node -v
npm -v
```

Step 2 Create a New React App

The easiest way to set up a React project is by using Create React App

Run the following command in your terminal

```sh
npx create-react-app my-app
```

This will create a new directory called my-app with all the necessary files and dependencies installed

Navigate into the project folder

```sh
cd my-app
```

Step 3 Start the Development Server

Run the following command to start the local development server

```sh
npm start
```

This will open http://localhost:3000/ in your browser displaying the default React welcome page

Step 4 Understanding the Project Structure

When you open the my-app folder you'll see several important files

src

This is where your actual React code lives

public

Contains static assets like images and the main HTML file

packagejson

Lists dependencies and scripts for managing the project

Step 5 Creating Your First React Component

Inside the src folder create a new file called Hellojs and add the following code

```jsx
import React from "react"

function Hello() {
    return <h1>Hello World from React</h1>
}

export default Hello
```

Now open Appjs and replace the default code with

```jsx
import React from "react"
import Hello from "./Hello"
```

```
function App() {
  return (
    <div>
      <Hello />
    </div>
  )
}

export default App
```
```

Save the file and refresh your browser You should see Hello World from React displayed on the screen
```

Backend Development Basics

The backend of a web application is where the real magic happens It's the engine that powers everything behind the scenes handling data processing user authentication database operations and server-side logic. While the frontend is what users see and interact with the backend ensures that data is retrieved processed and stored properly

When you log into a website upload a photo or send a message you're interacting with the backend Every time a website dynamically updates content stores user preferences or retrieves search results it's because the backend is handling those requests and responding with the necessary data

What is a Backend

At its core the backend is responsible for three main tasks handling requests processing data and sending responses. When a user performs an action like submitting a form on a website the frontend sends a request to the backend which processes the request and interacts with the database if necessary before sending a response back to the frontend

The backend typically consists of three main components

The Server

A server is a computer or program that listens for and responds to requests from clients web browsers mobile apps or other services The backend runs on a server which can be a physical machine in a data center or a cloud-based instance hosted by providers like AWS Google Cloud or DigitalOcean

The Database

A database stores and manages data efficiently allowing the backend to retrieve and manipulate information when needed Examples of data stored in a database include user credentials product details orders and messages Popular databases include MongoDB PostgreSQL MySQL and Firebase.

The Application Logic

The application logic is the code that determines how the backend processes data It includes authentication algorithms business rules and communication with third-party APIs. The backend is responsible for ensuring that only authorized users can access certain data performing calculations validating inputs and much more

Introduction to Nodejs and Expressjs

Nodejs is a runtime environment that allows developers to run JavaScript on the backend instead of just in the browser It is fast scalable and efficient making it a popular choice for modern web applications

Why Use Nodejs for Backend Development

Single Programming Language Since both the frontend and backend can be written in JavaScript using Nodejs makes development seamless and efficient

Event-Driven and Non-Blocking. Unlike traditional backend languages that handle requests one at a time Nodejs uses an asynchronous event-driven architecture that allows it to handle multiple requests simultaneously making it ideal for real-time applications like chat apps and live notifications

Huge Ecosystem. Nodejs has a massive ecosystem of packages and libraries available via npm Node Package Manager making it easy to integrate features like authentication payment processing and database connections

Setting Up Nodejs

To get started with Nodejs install it from nodejsorg and verify the installation with

```sh
node -v
npm -v
```

Introduction to Expressjs

Expressjs is a lightweight and flexible web framework for Nodejs It simplifies backend development by providing tools for handling routes middleware and server responses

To install Expressjs in a Nodejs project run

```sh
npm install express
```

```
```

Creating a Simple Express Server

Create a file called serverjs and add the following code

```js
const express = require("express")
const app = express()

appget("/" (req res) => {
  ressend("Hello World from Express")
})

applisten(3000 () => {
  consolelog("Server is running on port 3000")
})
```

This code does the following

1 Loads the Express library

2 Creates an Express application

3 Defines a route **/** that sends a response when accessed

4 Starts the server on port 3000

Run the server with

```sh
node serverjs
```

Then visit http://localhost:3000/ in your browser to see Hello World from Express displayed

Connecting to Databases MongoDB PostgreSQL

Databases are an essential part of backend development allowing applications to store and retrieve data efficiently Two of the most popular databases are MongoDB a NoSQL database and PostgreSQL a relational SQL database.

Connecting to MongoDB

MongoDB is a NoSQL database that stores data in JSON-like documents instead of tables making it flexible and scalable It's commonly used with Nodejs applications and integrates well with Mongoose a library for handling MongoDB operations.

nstalling and Setting Up MongoDB

1 Install MongoDB from mongodbcom
2 Install Mongoose in your Nodejs project

```sh
npm install mongoose
```

```
```

Connecting to MongoDB

In serverjs add the following code to establish a connection

```js
const mongoose = require("mongoose")

mongooseconnect("mongodb://localhost:27017/mydatabase" {
  useNewUrlParser true
  useUnifiedTopology true
})
then(() => consolelog("Connected to MongoDB"))
catch(err => consoleerror("Error connecting to MongoDB" err))
```

Defining a Model and Adding Data

A model defines the structure of a document in MongoDB Let's create a simple User model

```js
const UserSchema = new mongooseSchema({
  name String
  email String
  age Number
```

```
})

const User = mongoosemodel("User" UserSchema)

const newUser = new User({
  name "Alice"
  email "alice@examplecom"
  age 25
})

newUsersave()
then(() => consolelog("User saved"))
catch(err => consoleerror("Error saving user" err))
```

This creates a User collection in MongoDB and inserts a document with name email and age fields

Connecting to PostgreSQL

PostgreSQL is a relational SQL database that stores data in tables with predefined schemas. Unlike MongoDB which is flexible PostgreSQL enforces structure making it ideal for applications that require complex queries and data relationships

Installing PostgreSQL and Nodepg

First install PostgreSQL and then install the pg package for Nodejs

```sh
npm install pg
```

Connecting to PostgreSQL

In serverjs set up a connection to PostgreSQL

```js
const { Client } = require("pg")

const client = new Client({
  user "postgres"
  host "localhost"
  database "mydatabase"
  password "mypassword"
  port 5432
})

clientconnect()
then(() => consolelog("Connected to PostgreSQL"))
catch(err => consoleerror("Error connecting to PostgreSQL" err))
```

Creating a Table and Adding Data

Create a users table in PostgreSQL

```js
clientquery(`CREATE TABLE IF NOT EXISTS users (
  id SERIAL PRIMARY KEY
  name VARCHAR(100)
  email VARCHAR(100) UNIQUE
  age INT
)`)
then(() => consolelog("Table created"))
catch(err => consoleerror("Error creating table" err))
```

Insert a user into the table

```js
clientquery(`INSERT INTO users (name email age) VALUES ($1 $2 $3)`
  ["Alice" "alice@examplecom" 25])
then(() => consolelog("User added"))
catch(err => consoleerror("Error inserting user" err))
```

Choosing Between MongoDB and PostgreSQL

Use MongoDB if your application requires flexible schemas fast development and scalability. MongoDB is great for real-time applications like chat apps and content management systems

Use PostgreSQL if you need structured data complex queries and strong data relationships PostgreSQL is best for applications like banking systems enterprise software and analytical tools.

Deploying Your Website

After spending time developing your website locally the next step is to make it accessible to the world This is where deployment comes in

Deploying a website means publishing your code and making it available online so that anyone with an internet connection can visit it Whether you've built a simple HTML page or a complex JavaScript web application you'll need a hosting service to store and serve your files

Before diving into deployment methods let's look at the different hosting options available and the key factors to consider when choosing a hosting provider

Hosting Options Free vs Paid

Web hosting services come in two main categories free hosting and paid hosting Choosing between them depends on factors like website complexity traffic needs and required features

Free Hosting

Free hosting platforms are a great option for small projects personal portfolios and beginner websites These services allow you to publish your website without any upfront costs but they often come with limitations

Benefits of Free Hosting

- No Cost – Ideal for beginners who want to experiment without spending money
- Easy to Set Up – Most free hosting services have simple deployment processes
- Custom Domains Possible – Some allow you to connect your own domain instead of using a subdomain

Limitations of Free Hosting

- Limited Storage and Bandwidth – Free plans usually come with restrictions on file size and traffic
- No Backend Support – Most free hosting options only support static websites HTML CSS JavaScript and don't allow server-side code like Nodejs or databases
- Advertisements or Branding – Some free hosts display their branding on your site unless you upgrade
- Limited Customization – Features like SSL security and analytics may require paid upgrades

Best Free Hosting Services

- GitHub Pages – Great for hosting static websites directly from a GitHub repository
- Netlify – Simple drag-and-drop interface with continuous deployment from GitHub

- Vercel – Optimized for JavaScript frameworks like React and Nextjs offering fast performance

Paid Hosting

Paid hosting services offer more control performance and flexibility making them ideal for professional websites business applications and dynamic web apps with databases

Benefits of Paid Hosting

- More Storage and Bandwidth – Handles higher traffic and larger files
- Custom Domain and SSL Included – Ensures a professional and secure website
- Support for Backend and Databases – Allows for dynamic features like authentication and user accounts
- Better Performance – Faster servers and caching options for improved speed

Best Paid Hosting Services

- Bluehost SiteGround DreamHost – Traditional web hosts offering WordPress and full-stack hosting
- DigitalOcean Linode AWS EC2 – Cloud-based hosting for scalable applications
- Heroku Railway Render – Ideal for backend applications with database support

Deploying with GitHub Pages Netlify and Vercel

Now that we've covered hosting options let's look at how to deploy a website using three of the most popular free hosting services GitHub Pages Netlify and Vercel

Deploying with GitHub Pages

GitHub Pages is a free hosting service that allows you to deploy static websites HTML CSS JavaScript directly from a GitHub repository

Step 1 Push Your Project to GitHub

Create a GitHub account if you don't already have one at githubcom
Install Git on your computer if it's not installed
Initialize a Git repository in your project folder

```sh
git init
git add .
git commit -m "Initial commit"
```

Push the project to GitHub

```sh
git remote add origin https://github.com/your-username/your-repo.git
```

```
git branch -M main
git push -u origin main
```

Step 2 Enable GitHub Pages

Go to your repository on GitHub

Click on Settings

Scroll down to Pages

Under Source select main branch

Click Save

After a few minutes your site will be available at https://your-username.github.io/your-repo/

Deploying with Netlify

Netlify offers free and fast hosting with continuous deployment making it a great choice for frontend projects

Step 1 Sign Up for Netlify

Go to netlifycom and sign up using GitHub

Click New Site from Git

Choose your GitHub repository and branch

Step 2 Configure Deployment

Netlify will detect your project settings automatically

If your project is static just click Deploy Site

If using a framework like React enter the build command and publish directory

For React use

Build Command npm run build

Publish Directory build/

Step 3 Site Goes Live

After deployment Netlify provides a free subdomain like your-site.netlify.app You can also connect a custom domain

Deploying with Vercel

Vercel is designed for React Nextjs and modern JavaScript applications offering serverless functions automatic scaling and fast performance

Step 1 Sign Up for Vercel

Go to vercelcom and sign up using GitHub

Click New Project and select your repository

Step 2 Configure Deployment

Vercel automatically detects your framework settings

For React use

Build Command npm run build

Output Directory build/

Click Deploy

Step 3 Site Goes Live

Once deployed Vercel provides a subdomain like your-project.vercel.app You can also connect a custom domain

Setting Up a Custom Domain

Having a custom domain name makes your website look professional Instead of using a subdomain like your-site.netlify.app or your-repo.github.io you can use yourdomaincom

Step 1 Buy a Domain

Purchase a domain from a domain registrar like

Namecheap

GoDaddy

Google Domains

Cloudflare Registrar

Step 2 Configure DNS

Once you've purchased a domain you need to update its DNS settings to point to your hosting provider

Adding a Custom Domain to Netlify

Go to your Netlify dashboard

Select your deployed site

Click Domain Settings → Add Custom Domain

Enter your domain name and follow the DNS instructions

Adding a Custom Domain to Vercel

Open your Vercel project

Click Settings → Domains

Enter your domain name and follow the DNS setup guide

Updating DNS Records

If your hosting provider gives you nameservers update them in your domain registrar's settings If you're using A Records or CNAME Records update them accordingly

Step 3 Enable HTTPS with SSL

Most hosting providers automatically enable SSL certificates but if not enable it manually to ensure your site is secure and accessible via https:// instead of http://

Once your website is deployed and configured with a custom domain it is officially live and accessible worldwide.

Web Development Best Practices

Creating a website is not just about making it visually appealing It must be clean accessible secure and optimized for both users and search engines Following best practices ensures that your website is easy to maintain performs well ranks higher in search results and provides a great experience for everyone

Let's explore three critical areas of web development best practices writing clean and maintainable code accessibility and SEO basics and security essentials

Writing Clean and Maintainable Code

Writing clean code is one of the most important aspects of web development Good code is easy to read debug and update whether you or someone else is working on it later Messy unorganized code can make future improvements difficult and lead to hard-to-find bugs and performance issues

Follow Proper Naming Conventions

Naming variables functions and classes clearly helps make your code more readable Instead of using vague names like x or data use descriptive ones that reflect the purpose of the variable or function

Bad Example

```js
let x = 10
function doThing() {
  return x * 2
}
```

Good Example

```js
let itemPrice = 10
function calculateTotalPrice(price) {
  return price * 2
}
```

Using meaningful names helps developers instantly understand what the code is doing

Keep Your Code DRY Don't Repeat Yourself

Repeating code makes maintenance difficult If you find yourself copying and pasting the same lines multiple times refactor the code into reusable functions or components

Bad Example

```js
let price = 20
let tax = price * 01
let total = price + tax

let anotherPrice = 50
let anotherTax = anotherPrice * 01
let anotherTotal = anotherPrice + anotherTax
```

Good Example

```js
function calculateTotal(price) {
  let tax = price * 01
  return price + tax
}

let total1 = calculateTotal(20)
let total2 = calculateTotal(50)
```

Refactoring repeated code into a function makes the program easier to maintain and reduces the risk of errors

Use Comments Wisely

Comments should explain why something is done rather than what the code does If your code is self-explanatory excessive comments are unnecessary

Bad Example

```js
let p = 100 // Setting the price to 100
```

Good Example

```js
// Base price of the product before tax and discount
let basePrice = 100
```

Format and Indent Properly

Consistent indentation and spacing make your code easier to read Many developers use tools like Prettier or ESLint to automatically format their code

Accessibility and SEO Basics

Web accessibility and SEO Search Engine Optimization go hand in hand An accessible website ensures that everyone including people with disabilities can navigate and interact with it effectively At the same time search engines favor websites that are well-structured and user-friendly

Make Your Website Keyboard-Friendly

Some users rely on a keyboard or screen reader instead of a mouse to navigate your site Ensuring that all interactive elements like buttons links and forms can be accessed using the Tab key is crucial

```html
<button>Click Me</button>
```

Instead of using a div styled as a button use the correct HTML element so it is automatically keyboard-accessible

Bad Example

```html
<div onclick="doSomething()">Click Me</div>
```

```
```

Good Example

```html
<button onclick="doSomething()">Click Me</button>
```

Use Alt Text for Images

Screen readers rely on alt text to describe images If an image is purely decorative use alt="" to ensure it is ignored by assistive technologies

```html
<img src="mountainsjpg" alt="Snow-covered mountains under a bright blue sky">
```

Use Proper HTML Structure

A well-structured page helps both search engines and users navigate your site Use semantic HTML tags to give meaning to content

Bad Example

```html
<div class="header">
  <div class="title">Welcome to My Website</div>
```

```
</div>
```
```

**Good Example**

```html
<header>
  <h1>Welcome to My Website</h1>
</header>
```

Search engines and assistive technologies understand that h1 is the main heading which improves both SEO and accessibility

Improve Website Speed

A slow website affects both user experience and search engine rankings Some ways to improve speed include

Compress images using tools like TinyPNG or ImageOptim

Minimize CSS and JavaScript using minification tools

Use lazy loading for images and videos

Enable browser caching to load pages faster on repeat visits
```

Security Essentials

Security is one of the most critical aspects of web development Hackers constantly look for vulnerabilities and failing to secure your site can lead to data breaches malware infections and loss of user trust

Always Use HTTPS

HTTPS encrypts data transferred between users and your website protecting sensitive information like passwords and credit card details Most hosting providers offer free SSL certificates to enable HTTPS

```html
<a href="https://mywebsitecom">Secure Link</a>
```

Validate User Input

Never trust user input directly If your website has forms or login fields validate the input on both the client side JavaScript and server side backend to prevent attacks like SQL injection and cross-site scripting XSS

Bad Example

```js
let username = prompt("Enter your username")
```

```
documentwrite("Welcome " + username)
```

Good Example

```js
let username = prompt("Enter your username")
let safeUsername = usernamereplace(/</g, "&lt;")replace(/>/g, "&gt;")
documentwrite("Welcome " + safeUsername)
```

Sanitizing input prevents users from injecting harmful code

Protect Against Cross-Site Scripting XSS

XSS attacks happen when attackers inject malicious scripts into your website This
often happens when user-generated content is displayed without proper sanitization

Use frameworks like React or Vue which automatically escape user input
If using plain JavaScript sanitize all input before displaying it

Secure API Endpoints

If your website interacts with an API ensure that only authorized requests can access
data

Bad Example Exposing API keys in frontend JavaScript

```js
fetch("https://apiexamplecom/data?api_key=YOUR_SECRET_KEY")
```

Good Example Use environment variables and server-side authentication

```js
fetch("/get-data")
```

On the backend the request will include the API key securely without exposing it to users

Keep Software and Dependencies Updated

Outdated software and libraries can have security vulnerabilities Regularly update

Web frameworks React Vue Angular
Backend technologies Nodejs Express Django
Dependencies in packagejson or requirementstxt

Use tools like Dependabot or npm audit to identify security vulnerabilities in your dependencies

Next Steps in Web Development

Now that you've started your journey in web development it's time to think about how to take your skills to the next level As you grow your knowledge and experience you will encounter exciting opportunities for advancement Whether you want to learn more advanced JavaScript dive into full-stack development or explore potential career paths in web development there is always room for growth

Let's dive into some key next steps you can take to continue progressing in web development

Learning Advanced JavaScript

While the basics of JavaScript are essential to understanding web development there's much more to discover as you go deeper into the language The more advanced features of JavaScript will not only make your code more efficient but will also allow you to handle complex tasks like working with APIs managing data flows and building more interactive dynamic applications

Async/Await

One of the most powerful tools introduced in modern JavaScript is async/await This feature allows you to work with asynchronous code in a way that's more readable and easier to follow than using traditional callbacks or promises Async/await makes it simple to work with APIs fetch data from servers or perform tasks that take time without blocking the rest of your application

Here's an example of using async/await to fetch data from an API

```js
async function getData() {
  try {
    const response = await fetch('https://api.example.com/data')
    const data = await response.json()
    console.log(data)
  } catch (error) {
    console.error('Error fetching data', error)
  }
}

getData()
```

With async/await you get a cleaner syntax without having to chain `.then()` and `.catch()` as you do with traditional promises This makes your asynchronous code look almost like synchronous code

Promises

Before async/await the common way to handle asynchronous operations was through promises A promise represents a value that might be available now or in the future after an asynchronous operation has completed

Here's an example using promises to handle data from an API

```js
fetch('https://api.example.com/data')
  .then(response => response.json())
  .then(data => console.log(data))
  .catch(error => console.error('Error fetching data', error))
```

Although promises still work perfectly fine async/await is often preferred for its cleaner and more readable syntax Especially when dealing with multiple asynchronous calls that depend on each other

Exploring Full-Stack Development

While front-end development focuses on what users see and interact with full-stack development allows you to work on both the front-end and the back-end of a website or application Full-stack developers have a broader skill set that involves learning both client-side technologies (HTML CSS JavaScript) and server-side technologies (Node.js Express.js databases)

What is Full-Stack Development?

A full-stack developer works on both the front-end (the user interface) and the back-end (the server-side code and database) This allows you to build and manage a complete web application from start to finish A typical full-stack developer is proficient in the following areas

- Front-end: HTML CSS JavaScript frameworks like React or Vue
- Back-end: Server-side languages like Node.js Python or Ruby and frameworks like Express.js or Django
- Databases: Knowledge of how to store data using databases like MongoDB MySQL or PostgreSQL

Here's an example of how full-stack development might work in practice
1. The front-end of a website is built using HTML CSS and JavaScript which the user interacts with
2. The back-end involves creating a server with Node.js and Express.js to handle requests from the front-end
3. The back-end is connected to a database like MongoDB to store and retrieve data

Tools and Technologies

- Node.js: A JavaScript runtime built on Chrome's V8 engine that allows you to write server-side code using JavaScript
- Express.js: A minimalist framework for building web applications on Node.js
- Databases: Full-stack developers need to know how to interact with databases such as MongoDB (NoSQL) or PostgreSQL (SQL)
- APIs: Full-stack development often involves integrating third-party APIs or building your own API to handle requests between the front-end and back-end

If you're ready to dive into full-stack development start by learning Node.js and Express.js for the back-end while continuing to improve your front-end skills with

React or Vue This will give you the ability to create and manage both the client and server-side of your web applications

Career Paths and How to Get a Web Dev Job

As a web developer you have a variety of career paths to explore The field of web development is constantly evolving so it's essential to stay current with the latest tools and technologies Whether you want to work as a front-end developer back-end developer full-stack developer or specialize in other areas like UX/UI design or mobile development there are many opportunities available

Front-End Developer

A front-end developer specializes in creating the visual elements of a website and making sure the website functions properly on the user's device This involves using HTML CSS and JavaScript as well as front-end frameworks like React or Vue

To become a front-end developer you should focus on mastering HTML CSS and JavaScript Learn about responsive design cross-browser compatibility and performance optimization

Back-End Developer

A back-end developer works on the server-side of a website This includes building and maintaining the server that hosts the website and interacting with databases to manage data Back-end developers often use languages like Node.js Python Ruby or PHP

If you're interested in back-end development start by learning a server-side language and familiarize yourself with frameworks like Express.js for Node.js or Django for Python Then learn how to connect and interact with databases like MongoDB or PostgreSQL

Full-Stack Developer

A full-stack developer works on both the front-end and the back-end of a web application This allows them to build complete web applications from start to finish Full-stack developers often need to master both front-end technologies (HTML CSS JavaScript React Vue) and back-end technologies (Node.js Express.js databases)

Full-stack developers are in high demand because they can handle both the client and server-side of an application Start by learning front-end technologies and gradually move into back-end development

How to Get a Web Development Job

Getting a web development job requires a combination of learning the necessary technical skills and showcasing those skills through a portfolio and real-world projects

Here are some tips to help you get started

1. Build a Portfolio: Create your own website or web application to showcase your skills Include projects that demonstrate your ability to solve real problems and build functional websites

2. Contribute to Open Source: Open-source projects provide an excellent opportunity to gain experience and collaborate with other developers Look for projects on GitHub that need help and contribute to them

3. Networking: Join web development communities online or in person Attend meetups participate in forums or contribute to Slack groups and Discord servers

4. Internships and Freelance Work: If you're just starting out internships or freelance work are great ways to gain experience and build your resume Even if you don't have a lot of experience there are plenty of opportunities for entry-level positions

5. Keep Learning: Web development is always evolving Stay updated with the latest technologies frameworks and best practices by reading blogs attending workshops and completing online courses

By following these steps and continually improving your skills you'll be well on your way to landing your first job as a web developer

www.ingramcontent.com/pod-product-compliance
Lightning Source LLC
LaVergne TN
LVHW081759050326
832903LV00027B/2019